THE SCIENCE PLAYGROUND

Fun With Science Concepts & Nature

AuthorHouse™
1663 Liberty Drive
Bloomington, IN 47403
www.authorhouse.com
Phone: 833-262-8899

Because of the dynamic nature of the Internet, any web addresses or links contained in this book may have changed
since publication and may no longer be valid. The views expressed in this work are solely those of the author and do not
necessarily reflect the views of the publisher, and the publisher hereby disclaims any responsibility for them.

This book is printed on acid-free paper.

ISBN: 978-1-4389-3466-2 (sc)

Print information available on the last page.

Published by AuthorHouse 02/15/2022

authorHOUSE®

Contents

Sun Shares His Light

Sun asked Moon, "Why are you so sad?"

"I don't shine like you do. I have no light of my own" said Moon.

5

Moon shines happily at night in Sun's light.

Sun shines in its own light during the day.

Science Fact:

Sun has its own light while the moon shines due to the light that it reflects from the sun.

Moral/Social responsibility:

Friendship involves caring for one another and understanding each other's pain.

The Rainbow

There were seven kids in the Sunlight family –
Violet, Indigo, Blue, Green, Yellow, Orange and Red.

These kids were always huddled together tightly;
no one could tell they were seven different kids.

Their favorite game was playing on the water slide.

The water slide usually appeared on rainy days.

After it had stopped raining, the kids would rush out and jump on the water slide.

The water slide was long and slippery. The Kids would be thrown in different directions....

....each landing on a separate spot.

When you could see all the Sunlight Kids separately, they made a beautiful rainbow.

Science/Nature Fact:

White sunlight actually consists of seven colored lights which are not normally visible. When white light passes through a different medium (water, prism etc.) it bends (refraction) and separates out (dispersion). When we see all the colored lights separately we call the phenomenon a "Rainbow.

Moral Takeaway:

Just as the seven colors remain inseparable in normal sunlight, our society should always be united regardless of the cultural and racial diversities that we see. We should celebrate this diversity in our society because it is as beautiful as the Rainbow.

Earth and Sun Dance

Earth wants to dance with the Sun.

Sun says, "I cannot dance." He feels sad.

Earth says, "No problem. I will dance all around you. You can watch me dance."

Earth wants to make her dance fun. She says, "I will have three steps in my dance."

First, Earth runs around the Sun. This makes Sun happy.

Second, Earth also spins as she runs around the Sun. This makes Sun even happier.

Third, Earth does not stay straight. She tilts as she spins and runs around the Sun.

By now Sun is so happy that he forgets that he cannot dance.

Earth says, "Hey look! As I spin I am causing day and night. When I face you Sun, I have day and when my back is towards you it's night."

Sun says, "Yes, and your tilting and running around me is causing four different seasons."

Science Fact:

The Earth moves around the Sun, while the Sun is stationary. This story explains how the Rotation of the earth causes day & night, while Revolution around the sun causes seasons in a year.

Moral/Social responsibility:

Many individuals in society are differently abled. They may not be able to participate in some of the activities that others can. We should be understanding and think of ways to include them as much as possible and spread happiness around.

Tree and Creeper

Once there was a tree. The gigantic tree stood alone in the middle of a large empty field. He felt great pride in being big and mighty, but he also felt very lonely.

One hot sunny day, the tree saw a traveler approaching. The tree felt very happy.

The traveler stopped to take shelter under the tree.

He ate some fruits, tied the bull to the tree and took a short nap. Some seeds had dropped on the ground while he ate.

The traveler soon left. The tree was lonely again and felt sad.

After a few days, the tree noticed a small green thing creeping up on him.

The tree got scared. "Is it a snake?" he thought.

After a few days, the creeper grew taller. She started winding itself around the mighty tree.

The tree felt the warmth of the creeper and felt very happy. They soon became good friends.

The creeper grew big and started blooming.

Soon, the flowers started attracting birds,
butterflies and other creatures.

The mighty tree gave the creeper the support she needed. The creeper, in turn, provided the tree with the friendship that it had been craving for so long.

They were both very happy.

Nature Fact:

Some creepers grow along trees and get support from the tree that they climb along. The biological interaction in which plants from different species benefit from each other is called mutualism.

Social responsibility:

In any family (or society), one can see how we all depend on each other – each member provides comfort and support to the other members. Harmony in families and society is essential for developing sound personalities.

Printed in the United States
by Baker & Taylor Publisher Services